Bad Dogs

Bad Dogs

John S.P. Walker

Alfred A. Knopf   New York   1982

Copyright © 1976, 1977, 1978, 1979, 1980, 1981, 1982
by John S. P. Walker
All rights reserved under International and Pan-American
Copyright Conventions. Published in the United States by
Alfred A. Knopf, Inc., New York, and simultaneously in Canada
by Random House of Canada Limited, Toronto.
Distributed by Random House, Inc., New York.

Some of these drawings were originally seen in Esquire,
National Lampoon, Soho Weekly News, and Fire Island News.

Designed by Virginia Tan

Library of Congress Cataloging in Publication Data
Walker, John S. P. [date] Bad Dogs
1. Dogs—Caricatures and cartoons. 2. American
wit and humor, Pictorial. I. Title.
NC1429.W22A4 1982   741.5'973   81-11768
ISBN 0-394-52213-3   AACR2

Manufactured in the United States of America
First Edition

For Mad "Gordon Lish" Dog

Special thanks to Burt Britton, George Booth,
Nora Ephron, Harold Hayes, Adele Hoenig, Peter Kleinman,
Nancy Lindbloom, George Mazzei, The Andersons,
and, especially, The Folks.

Bad Dogs

Famed inventor Ian McLeachey with new electric cat

Idiot dogs being driven home

Lucius Carp spills his guts

Man caught in the act of cat-hurling

New breed of consumer dog

Contest winners enjoying free dance lesson

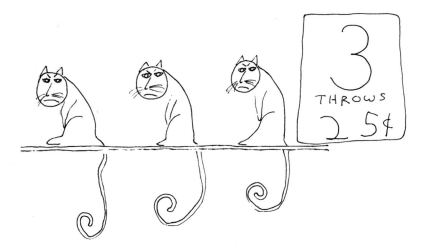

Cats down on their luck

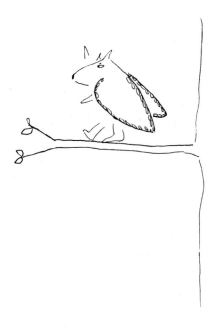

Brilliant dog testing invention

Lowell Creach waits for the money to roll in

Chorus dogs

Fish Dating Service

Cat having grand time at a party

One of four genius birds in captivity

Pancho Gonzales eaten by leprechauns
at Wimbledon

Transit worker with shoe trees
anxious for use of record booth as he is only on short break

Proud king with new prince

Proud king with new prince with new hairstyles

Cats with a grave misunderstanding of the situation

Conceptual artist changing mind
and throwing out flies

Persian heir enjoying a trampoline

Olympic dog beset by sudden loss of confidence

Bronson Daniels, ordering two more,

being mocked by his dog, Leonard

Dog over-zealously guarding piece of junk mail

Chance encounter with extraterrestrials

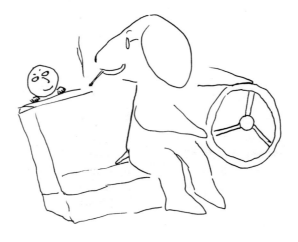

Veteran cab driver regaling a passenger

Extremely rare cat being delivered by public transport

Julio Larsen explains the concept of "weather"

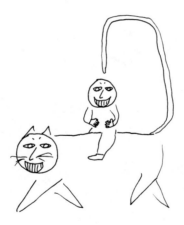

Cat trying to signal he is being kidnapped

Dog trying to recover his license

Deranged cat forced to sell his collection

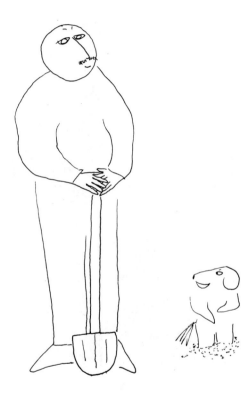

Gardener and dog in joke pose

Telekinetic kid showing off

Raymond Fielding describing one of
the truly great moments in his life

Horse hustled into giving heavy dogs a ride to the airport

Owner of goat bar serving his first customer

The cunning Hollis Lee on verge of capturing alligator

Fanatic leading a national dog revolt

Rudy Garcia becomes privy to a secret

Dog looking for high adventure

Daredevil being launched into a bucket

Dog absolutely positive he's on his way to First Class

Drowning man not wanting to be a bother

Lars Doyle prepares to light the ceremonial goat

The man with all the answers

Bud Parker psychs out the competition

Man successfully levitating cat

Cat successfully levitating himself

Spies hard at work

Rich gypsy bowling in his own home

The Return of The Cat Hammerer

Fox under the impression he is working in a factory

Last year's winner

Roy Shower exercises extremely poor judgment

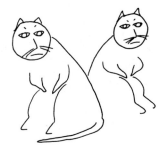

Cats soured on life after missing the Rolling Stones

Amateur magician with volunteer

Solicitous dog with dinner guest

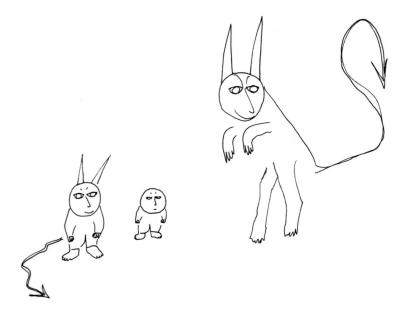

Lyle Finch's first exposure to demons

Marriage counselor exhibiting most recent success

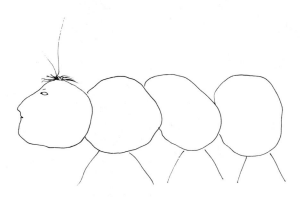

Ant worrying about his responsibilities

Charles Hobsburn reacts to his dog's sudden outcry

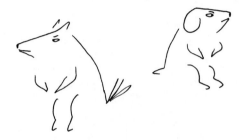

Dog-Juggling Time

Cat and fish enduring cultural exchange

Two winners

Deaf cats trying to follow dubbed film

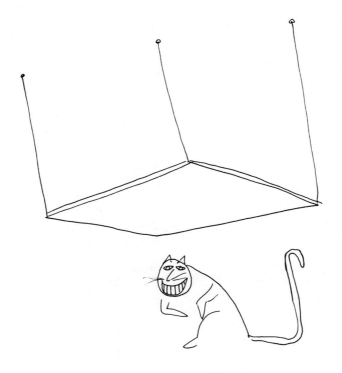

Cat face to face with disaster

The last known photo of Dr. Colin Jerome

Phil Miller demonstrates The World's Fastest Dog

Gourmet goat preparing to enjoy rack of Chilled Guitar

Paul Grub misses the early bird by five minutes

The Rupert Triplets' first telepathic experience

Dog indulging in a luxury

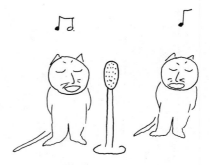

Cats running overtime on live t.v.

Alligator reveling in Strother Martin festival

Close-knit family

Dogs unimpressed by priceless antique bureau

New neighbors hitting it off

The Loch Ness Formal

Lester Davis forced to pass up a bargain

Dog virtually getting away with murder

Cat entering second phase
of elaborate plan to get Japanese food

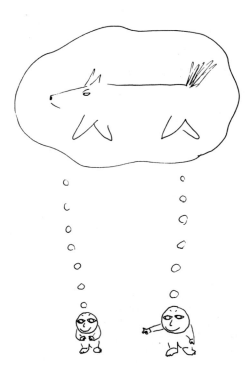

Babies greatly excited by what
they perceive to be a cat

Cat entering second phase
of elaborate plan to get Japanese food

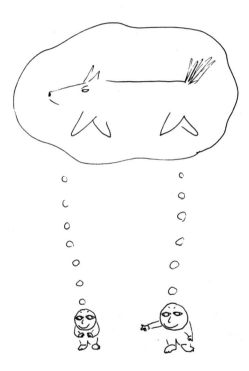

Babies greatly excited by what
they perceive to be a cat

Uncle Henry cheating at ring-toss

Diplomat from the Animal Kingdom

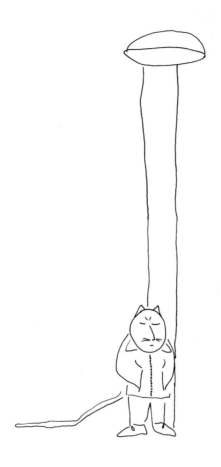

Cat profoundly influenced by James Dean

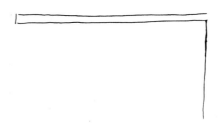

Contest winner jumping into a vat of dog food

Shrewd cat preparing for the season

Psychics on the verge of winning a dishwasher

Dog's cover blown by romantic

Dog with the general idea

Robert Wyatt discovers chunk of ice on his deep-pile carpet

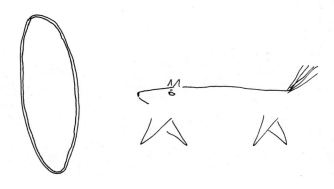

Dog taking civil-service examination

Fox plotting to change places with flower

Eddie Chamberlain goes to greet his guests

Dog admiring recent ear-bob

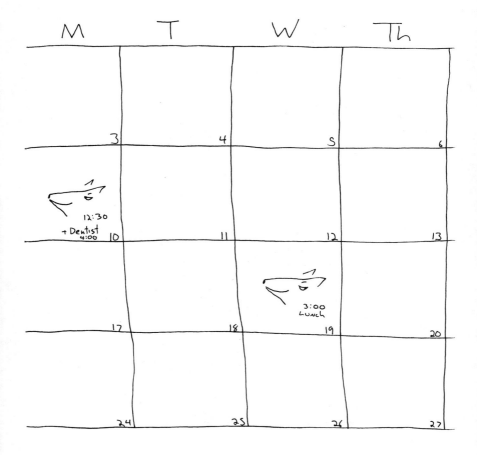

Young lad left alone for ten seconds

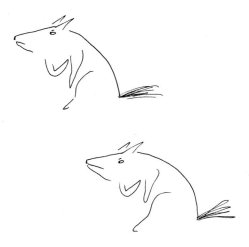

Dogs preparing for brutal competition

Young lad left alone for ten seconds

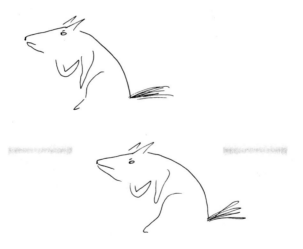

Dogs preparing for brutal competition

Lloyd Otis notices a cow advancing in his direction

Idiot dog sealing his fate

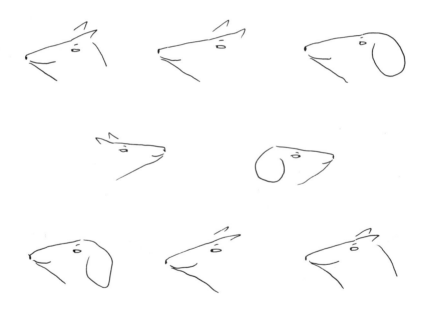

Obedience School Class Photo

Jack Turner puts the trout through their paces

Young psychic torn between watching
television and reading cat's mind

Conservative stunned by his dog's cultural advances

Dogs believing they've stumbled onto a good thing

First fish to get a good look at the moon

The Last Resort of the Dog Artist

About the Author

John S. P. Walker was born in New York City
on April 9, 1954. He hopes to continue residence
in the place of his birth.